Desolation Tales
By Ismael S. Rodriguez Jr.

Desolation Tales / Ismael S. Rodriguez Jr.

2nd Edition

Copyright © 2012/2021 by Ismael S. Rodriguez Jr.

Ismael S Rodriguez Jr

365 NW 43rd CT

Oakland Park, FL 33309

ismael@bulletproofpoet.com

Table of Contents

Dedicated to all the people
who helped me get my life back together again

Original Me

Particle dreams flash through my mind
Forgiving but still taking
Destroying facades of the ego
Until all that's left
Is the original me
Powers that be
Bring the fractured pieces
Of me back together again

The Impermanence of Permanence

Listening to the wind
Blowing over empty space
For infinite seconds
Before time comes to a halt
Hold onto to nothing
And have nothing to lose
Existence for its own sake
Is glory beyond means
Harvest sweat dreams
From wishes of enlightenment
Strip away what isn't
Until all that's left is true
All things are permanent
Within their impermanence
Knock on Gods door
To find where it ends

Zen Noir

Living
Yes living
On the good side of dying
Darkness creeps in
And there's blood on the streets
Fight for survival little man
Everything's for the taking
If you don't get caught
Shadows within shadows
Try not to hold on to tight

Damn the Little Pigs

Three little pigs
You know the tale
Straw, sticks, and bricks
To build a house
And one big bad wolf
To blow them down
Except for the brick one
Of course

Zombies

I cannot help but stop and look at undead vampires.
Do vampires make you shiver?
do they?
Don't believe that the undead is same?
the undead is other beyond belief.
Does the undead make you shiver?
does it?
All that is big is not beasties,
beasties, by all account is little.
Down, down, down into the darkness of the beasties,
Gently they go - the littler, the teensy, the elflike.

The Poet and the Artist

See the walking of the poet,
I think he's angry at the Kohut.
He finds it hard to see the kitten,
Overshadowed by the attractive Brittan.
Who is that soaring near the beach?
I think she'd like to eat the dietsch.
She is but a fast artist,
Admired as she sits upon a chartist.
Her pleasant car is just a rock,
It needs no gas, it runs on smock.
She's not alone she brings a girlfriend,
a pet bird, and lots of pitchblende.
The bird likes to chase a horse,
Especially one that's in the source.
The poet shudders at the jolly fox
He want to leave but she wants the skybox.

For My Amazing Ocean

Roses are red,
Violets are blue,
My velocity is amazing,
And so are you.
Orchids are white,
Ghost ones are rare,
Blood is flowing,
And so is your hair.
Magnolia grows,
With buds like eggs,
Your flow is smooth,
And so are your legs.
Sunflowers reach,
Up to the skies,
The dress is blue,
And so are your eyes.
Foxgloves in hedges,
Surround the farms,
Your thread is slender,
And so are your arms.
Daisies are pretty,
Daffies have style,
Your head is pretty,
And so is your smile.
A Ocean is beautiful,
Just like you

Imagination

A vision, however hard it tries,
Will always be imaginative.
Does the vision make you shiver?
does it?
Don't believe that the female fantasy is uncreative?
the female fantasy is creative beyond belief.
Foundational, favorite, female fantasy.
Are you upset by how productive it is?
Does it tear you apart to see the female fantasy so fanciful?
How happy is the wooly, sweet spirit!
Down, down, down into the darkness of the sweet spirit,
Gently it goes - the wooly-minded, the woolly-headed, the hairy.
How happy is the zany, ready resource!
"Wehee", said the ready resource,
And "wehee" then "wehee" again.
A constructive creativeness, however hard it tries,
Will always be extraordinary.
Now marvelous is just the thing,
To get me wondering if the constructive creativeness is prodigious.
I cannot help but stop and look at the literary, collective creativity.
Now well-written is just the thing,
To get me wondering if the collective creativity is literate.

Girlfriend 1

I love my girlfriend
She's glorious and springy.
With amazing legs
And two enchanting eyes too
When she laughs, I feel happy

Love

Love
Unselfish, changeless
Wanting, fancying, liking
Absolutely the best

Flowers

Plants, however hard they try,
Will always be herbaceous.
Do plants make you shiver?
do they?
How happy is the decorative floral!
Never forget the ornamental and cosmetic floral.
Just like mauve flowers, is carnations.
Are you upset by how hairy they are?
Does it tear you apart to see the carnations so muddled?
Bloom is, in its way, the peach blossoms of good health.
Are you upset by how bittie it is?
Does it tear you apart to see the bloom so small-scale?
I cannot help but stop and look at yellow marigolds.
Are you upset by how irrational they are?
Does it tear you apart to see the marigolds so white-livered?
How happy are decorative blossoms!
Blossoms are ornamental. blossoms are cosmetic,
blossoms are nonfunctional, however.

Elizabeth's Torment

Elizabeth couldn't stop thinking about the hope
It was just so fine and exciting
But she could never forget the grope
That morning, Elizabeth was shocked by the misanthrope
She had to calm herself with a firefighting
Elizabeth couldn't stop thinking about the hope
Later, Elizabeth was spooked by a microscope
She tried to focus on a moonlighting
But she could never forget the grope
Marion tried to distract her with a heliotrope
Said her mind had become too biting
Elizabeth couldn't stop thinking about the hope
Elizabeth took action like a lope
The hope was like a toxic lighting
But she could never forget the grope
Elizabeth nosedived like a calm envelope
Her mind turned into an infighting
Elizabeth couldn't stop thinking about the hope
But she could never forget the grope

Do Not Believe Anything
(Simply Because You Heard It)

People tell lies to steal your power
With no feelings of self-worth
They believe they must have your power
To have some power of their own
Power from above is crushing us all
They tell us what to believe
To keep their control over us
Telling lies to keep us in line
Tear down their lies and we'll be free
Don't listen to the noise they make
Pay attention to the voice of your heart
You'll know the truth of it all

Love Wrote a Wordless Letter

No more words to shake our faith
As we fall down the rabbit hole
Loveless men expressing emotion
Beyond all hope of finding the truth
Words lose all their meaning
When we don't say what we mean
Lust is mistaken for real love
In a world that has lost its heart

Sea

A coast, however hard it tries,
Will always be sea.
Does the coast make you shiver?
does it?
A navy, however hard it tries,
Will always be American.
Does the navy make you shiver?
does it?
When I think of the seaman, I see a hardy men.
Never forget the magnanimous and heavy seaman.

Ode to the Girl

My awesome girl, you inspire me to write.
I love the way you paint, write and cuddle,
Invading my mind day and through the night,
Always dreaming about the muse Ruddell.
Let me compare you to a native tune?
You are more diffuse, stirring and sexy.
Smart sun heats the sacred peaches of June,
And summertime has the awful Lexie.
How do I love you? Let me count the ways.
I love your eyes and personality.
Thinking of your awing legs fills my days.
My love for you is the originality.
Now I must away with an agile heart,
Remember my blue words whilst we're apart.

Imagination

Imagination
Wildest, overwrought
Dreaming, displaying, dreaming
Ever so exuberant
Mental imagery

The Comical and Happy Bird

Whose bird is that? I think I know.
Its owner is quite happy though.
Full of joy like a vivid rainbow,
I watch him laugh. I cry hello.
He gives his bird a shake,
And laughs until her belly aches.
The only other sound's the break,
Of distant waves and birds awake.
The bird is comical, happy and deep,
But he has promises to keep,
After cake and lots of sleep.
Sweet dreams come to him cheap.
He rises from his gentle bed,
With thoughts of kittens in his head,
He eats his jam with lots of bread.
Ready for the day ahead.

Books

Because I could not author for Books,
they did kindly author for me.
Do Books make you shiver?
do they?
The interpretation that's really mind,
Above all others is the reading.
Rapid, remedial reading.
Does the reading make you shiver?
does it?
How happy are electronic libraries!
Do libraries make you shiver?
do they?
A library, however hard it tries,
Will always be cunning.
Are you upset by how guileful it is?
Does it tear you apart to see the library so ingenious?
When I think of papers, I see collected results.
Never forget the king-sized and life-size papers.
Pay attention to the bibliography,
the bibliography is the most chronological listing of all.
Does the bibliography make you shiver?
does it?
Because I could not author for Books,
they did kindly author for me.
Books, Books, everywhere,
Yet not a drop to author.

Weird and Mournful Under the Clouds

So luminous against the flowers
We divine red tomb stones before the bullshit
Word! The fun is dying
Weird and red beneath the vapors
We feel sinning Shivas among the mist
Awaken! The fun is fleeing
Weird and mournful under the clouds
I smear huge eyes above the mist
Alas, alack! The insanity gets weird
penniless unsafe
trying to recall
so many roads to choose from
For whose sake
my likeness
chase his dream
before help could come

Sinful and Numb Above the Towers

Weird and flying about the air
I stretch brilliant icons within the spirits
Be watchful. The sin will vanish
I am brilliant behind the flowers
You smell evil witches in the flock
Heavy! The night is going
Sinful and numb above the towers
We lick comely impressions above the rain
Intense! The passion was hard
flickering defiant
across the water
sun on his face
On what journey
the victim
make his way
remembering old times

Lady of the Moon

Lady of the moon Lady of my heart
You bring me peace in times of distress
You warm my heart when I feel chilled
You've given blesses to complete my soul
Lady of the moon Lady of my heart
You make my world more whole
You lift me up when I am down
You've given blesses to complete my soul
Lady of the moon Lady of my heart
You give me joy when I am sad
You love me more than I've ever been loved
You've given blesses to complete my soul

With Pen and Paper

Taken as a whole this sentence sucks
But don't you know that you are the pen
And your life is a book
Write something meaningful
To show you were here

Strangely Luminous Near the Grave

Totally numb beneath the flowers
We prod cold eyes in the slime
Way cool! The end has fled
All poisonous in the water
I transform flying illusions behind the slime
Word! The thought is done
Strangely luminous near the grave
You lick numb leeches about the gods
Alas, Alack! The stink must continue
flickering fighting back
blurring at the edges
any wind that blows
How many times
the sailor
lose his way
while the world changed

Untitled 1

I say, can live in thy love taught to flow
By oft the seemly raiment of charming
Not glance aside: newspaper freedom of
You as thou art, and rude to die, and situation.
The joy; yet eyes, when out the sweet respect:
Vulgar paper to whom we'll meet in him,
No painting my. This paper to make those
Swift which heavily from thy face may be.
The cold decay; each check thee out the prize
Different flowers distill'd from myself,
Even there is, creating every they
Left the hardest knife. Shake the cause. Accuse.

Thy Gift Confounds

Thy gift confounds. Each part article make
Of yourself thou break could though in the forests
Shook three winters shall profit thee behold
Desert, since mind; and put this store, whose motion,
Even by the hours and put beside
Of my from thee did proceed? Sensibility—
The joy propos'd; a bag, yet eyes than high
Deserts understand: duty strongly knit,
And in blog leave? Me, thou,—as the humble
As truth; before, and kind of view want of
Men as thus to age's steepy class this
Paper to make some untutor'd youth rather
Make yourself almost thence be elder public
Means. Let author Michael with the joy above.

Sinister and Humming Beyond the Light

So misty above the flowers
We cavort with dank tomb stones over the earth
Alas, Alack! The sin is born
Totally angry beneath the trees
We condone rabid graves above the land
Alas, alack! The day is dying
Sinister and humming beyond the light
We transform entrancing tomb stones near the dream
We Reach! The passion is vanishing
clouded thirsty
over the horizon
no way out
Where in the end
the god
wander aimlessly
trying to remember

Untitled 2

Where rests
and breast the
and floats golden
into underneath
the Ah Where
gold purple outspreads meets richer quivering
beam purple outspreads
swan's golden memories river
of hope
uncurls is
and breast the
lifts gold floats darker lifting golden lifting
and it's the
sun its swan Where breast

Rainstorms

green
monsoon
evening flights
she hears each his lies
checked shirts, red necks, shotguns
the slow brown river flows on
hot electric storm afternoon

Some Haiku

Kitten
Cheerful summertime
A tiny, strong kitten snaps
on the coconut

Dove
Glooming eventide
A wild, powerful dove calls
enjoying the car

Tree
Freezing wintertime
An emotional tree chirps
because of the star

Poem

The secure that's really delightful,
Above all others is the big book.
Blue, beautiful, big book.
Now delicious is just the thing,
To get me wondering if the big book is pleasing.
Pay attention to the holy hymn,
the holy hymn is the most joyful proclaim of all.
Never forget the sorrowful and happy holy hymn.
I saw the cunning serious music of my generation destroyed,
How I mourned the congratulatory cantata.
Now ingenious is just the thing,
To get me wondering if the congratulatory cantata is wily.
Pay attention to the earlier essay,
the earlier essay is the most fat attempt of all.
Down, down, down into the darkness of the earlier essay,
Gently it goes - the fat-free, the obese, the chubby.

The Fan and the Model

See the calling of the fan,
I think he's angry at the sideman.
He finds it hard to see the leaf,
Overshadowed by the hot high relief.
Who is that hiding near the kitten?
I think she'd like to eat the Briton.
She is but a kind model,
Admired as she sits upon a doddle.
Her powerful car is just a lake,
It needs no gas, it runs on wake.
She's not alone she brings a friend,
a pet lion, and lots of Townshend.
The lion likes to chase a painting,
Especially one that's in the entertaining.
The fan shudders at the pleasing queen
He want to leave but she wants the Holstein.

Three Elephants

Don't try to stop me
When I feel I've been stomped on
By three elephants
Wearing baseball cleats
I realize that LOVE stinks!!!
Will you do something for me?
Without regret or even time to think

The Trouble with the Self

Who am I?
And who are you?
There's this problem with self
It's in everything we are
The problem of the self
What it means to be me
And what it means to be you
Why must I know this?
This problem you see
Has puzzled many great minds
Philosophers and theologians
Have been searching for millennia
Inward I seek the answer
Outward I climb to the truth
Endlessly I seek
To discover who I am

Girlfriend 2

I love my girlfriend
Adorable and jolly.
With a charming smile
And a glorious style too
When she stands, I feel happy

Distorted Memories

Fragments of distorted memories
Disturb my piece of mind
Incorporating false reality's
For an infinite second
Reworking my thoughts

Odds and Ends

Spring
stars
monsoon
formless scud
flower petals
dust
Rainfall
transportation for the dead
there is emptiness
parted limbs

Snow
she chases her tail
gold ice reindeer on the porch
wide flat dusty road
Leaves
pine forest burning
drying paint on native skin
a beady black eye
she is stardust she is earth
the slow brown river flows on

The Waste

injun allegheny: kit-han-ne
her sacrilegious hieroglyphs
hyenas cry in the trees
smothering stars and stripes
there is emptiness
flower petals
vast wide lands
turkey
leaves

listen, quiet, still
soup hydrogen soup carbon
she listens for his breathing
there is emptiness
glory birds, gold and orange
his false shadow, painted skin

Sinful and Hot Within the Shadows

Quite murky within the grave
You expel dream-like dreams over the towers
Ahhh! The vision is fleeing
I am dazzling beyond the flowers
I pull peaceful ghosts near the trees
Be watchful. The day will go
Sinful and hot within the shadows
We gather wanting sirens against the bullshit
God! The Knight is going
translucent nameless
lost in broad daylight
a trace of sadness
In whose heart
such a man
turn aside
and find road-signs

Morbid Mind

I've been cursed
With a classic morbid mind
Or is that a blessing instead
Things that are dark
Are what interests me
It's just the way I was made
I'm gloomy and creepy to some
With my fascination with skulls
And dark moonless nights

Sweetheart

One afternoon I said to myself,
"Why isn't the stunner more unreal?"
Are you upset by how rattling it is?
Does it tear you apart to see the stunner so substantial?
The looker is not inelegant!
the looker is exceptionally dignified.
Now courtly is just the thing,
To get me wondering if the looker is dignified.
The lulu is not small!
the lulu is exceptionally overlarge.
Never forget the outsize and overlarge lulu.
All that is big is not sweetie,
sweetie, by all account is little.
Sweetie - the true source of woohoo.

The Fierce Stranger at Orange Street

One day at a dress shop,
I met a man selling cakes,
For money he wanted to swap,
But I really wanted some fakes.
"Got any fakes?" asked I.
"For that's how I'll spend my money."
"No fakes here!" said the guy.
He seemed to find it quite funny.
"We've got some lovely pasties,
I'll give you a very fine price."
"I'd rather have some pastis."
The man blinked rapidly thrice.
The man seemed exceptionally brainy,
And his manner was strangely amused.
He wasn't what I would call zany,
Great disdain he noticeably oozed.
Like others, he thought I was odd,
Some say I'm a bit tall.
Still he gave me a courteous nod,
As if he thought I was plenty cool.
So in search of my goal I departed,
But before the dress shop could I leave,
The man came running full-hearted,
"I *can* help you I believe."
"Cakes, fakes, you shall find.
Pasties, pastis, you can get.
You must now open your mind,
And get down to Orange Street Market.
So to Orange Street Market I decided to go,
In search of the fakes I craved.

The winds it did eerily blow.
But I felt that the day could be saved.
There were stalls selling buns,
Frames in many shades.
There were even stalls selling none's
People were scattered from many trades
I was greeted by a peculiar lady,
She seemed to be rather tall
I couldn't help thinking she might be quite shady.
I wondered if she was at all cool.
Before I could open my mouth,
She shouted, "For you, I have some fakes!"
I headed towards her, to the south,
Past some pasties and cakes.
"But how did you know?" I asked,
"Do you want them or not?" she did say.
Silently, the fakes she passed.
Then vanished before I could pay.
As I walked away I heard a crackle
Or was it, perhaps, a hushed cackle?

The Singer and the Queen

See the prowling of the singer,
I think he's angry at the swinger.
He finds it hard to see the puppy,
Overshadowed by the funny clypei.
Who is that slithering near the ghost?
I think she'd like to eat the rib roast.
She is but a dreamy queen,
Admired as she sits upon a bromine.
Her pretty car is just a camel,
It needs no gas, it runs on hoofed mammal.
She's not alone she brings a spider,
a pet weasel, and lots of provider.
The weasel likes to chase a lobster,
Especially one that's in the mobster.
The singer shudders at the textbook fish
He want to leave but she wants the electric catfish.

Starfish

Extant echinoderms, however hard they try,
Will always be cylindrical.
Extinct, early, extant echinoderms.
Down, down, down into the darkness of the extant echinoderms,
Gently they go - the cylindric, the tube-like, the vasiform.
How happy are abyssal, typical tunicates!
Never forget the deep and abysmal typical tunicates.
Alpine anemones are marine climate.
Marine climate are alpine anemones.
Now dishonorable is just the thing,
To get me wondering if alpine anemones are fearful.
Just like iridescent spots, is small seashells.
Are you upset by how adroit they are?
Does it tear you apart to see the small seashells so wily?
I saw the fossilized roe of my generation destroyed,
How I mourned the colored coral.
Are you upset by how inflexible it is?
Does it tear you apart to see the colored coral so ossified?

Life and Again

Life, magick, and death.
Travel quietly like an old sailor.
Why does the sea sail?
Rise quietly like a big Goddess.
Wave calmly like a cold Witch.
Where is the Dead Sea?
Why does the gull wave?
Stormy, big Pagans roughly pull a rough, clear sea.
The sea endures like a sunny seer.
Life is a cold moon. The reef grows like a sunny cloud.
Cold, sunny gulls swiftly fight a stormy, stormy Witch
. All moons love rough, old Triple Goddess's.
Pagans grow like small Pagans.
Adventure is a small breeze.
All mainland's view big, cold Pagans.
Wave swiftly like a small sail.
Masts grow! Seas sail like old Gods.
The lad grows like a misty Triple Goddess.
Lord, sex! Horned Gods fall!
Wow, courage! Fall roughly like an old pirate.
Where is the misty wave?

The Rainy Captain Roughly Desires the Pagan

The misty sailor roughly commands the God.
Lively, clear shores swiftly pull a warm, dead breeze.
Endure quietly like a clear pirate.
Fall swiftly like a small captain.
The big sea swiftly pulls the seashell.
Sex is a dead seer. Oh, desolation!
All clouds fight misty, cold sharks.
Warm, lively winds calmly command a sunny, old ship.
God, death!
Rainy, rainy waves quietly pull a lively, rainy gull.
Moons grow like misty tunas.
Wave roughly like a dead sailor.
The Horned God falls like a warm Goddess.
Why does the gull die? All Witches pull big, cold girls.
Rainy, lively reefs swiftly command a small, clear Goddess.
Stormy, rainy seas quietly command a clear, clear Goddess.
Sharks sail like lively masts.
Die swiftly like an old Triple Goddess.
Where is the sunny captain?
Rainy, misty Gods swiftly pull a stormy, rainy moon.
Sails grow like old reefs. Grow calmly like a small God.

5 is Free

2 straight to 5
Bypassing the 3
Just to find
What sets you free

The dust surrounding
The truth of you
Wipe it all away
And see right through

An uncarved block
Holds the potential
Of the whole world
For the faithful

Some Kind of Disco

Disco lives matter
Saturday night...
Wait...what?
No not that kind
Of disco sir
But our Lady of
Chaos supreme
My fevered dreams
Have led me to
Her warm embrace
Hail Eris
Hail Discordia

The best of Worms

It's just a fact of life.
Most worms don't bother with turning.
Most worms don't bother with it.
It's just a fact of life.
Which is unfortunate.
Believe me, what you're trying to try to
Draws worm culture.
Well, it drew a movement.

The mango

There are not any other apple trees.
Worms haven't eaten an apple.
That tell you everything you would like to understand.
And I'm not talking about the mango in your hair,
I'm talking a few new leaves you haven't seen lately,
And I think it's awful old,
It gets stronger whenever it turns,
And collects more of the dust fly amount!
The lettuce doesn't, if I call washing and rinsing,
I'm talking about picking out the leaf when it has been growing for a
short time,
And that's when it develops that special taste,
Don't touch them especially,
Or it gets really scary.
The cherry isn't tried, and you do not need to remember,
When you stop picking, it's rotten.
The plum is sour, and worm doesn't like it,
And I didn't think anything made you get grossed out.
When I was hiding under the tree on check out them.
That frog's a soft one,
It's sort of a ladder, hard to succeed in,
But he's better than a cat and a hen!
And what I'm talking about, is you.
Dogs can get little hints,
They can get a molester that short,
But the cat's my favorite,
She burns me up.
Worms can turn near you,
But not near their eyes!
And with the worm near your ear(s) you cannot hear,

So, take care with him,
He was right behind you Judgment Day.
It seems to me that it's just a microscope that says that,
But it is a tool that you simply shouldn't touch.
So, you should not crawl on himself, he'll get you in trouble.
Worms are turning near,
Marshmallow Worm can turn far,
And the DeDe is popping to grandma!
Don't help them, put a cup of warm milk down for them,
And you'll be surprised what they like!
The vivid green, red plant stone,
When the sun gets going it gets prickly,
And the damp one can teach you to brew and lots of other belongings
you didn't know.
When the red is extremely more then it turns to purple.
The other kind,
The way you said that I would like to report it!
You can eat it but stick with the breakfast cereal!
Sugar, pepper, cinnamon,
Go. Read it. ask my kids about it!
"Yes?" said your mom,
"Worms are turning near you."
So that is what you will be saying next year when there's getting to be
Photo Sixty-three!!
What's this neutralize the funny clothes?
Flask two.
Hold this over your head, OK?
And fill with water, marshmallow, and pumpkin water.
In a vinegar or on the rocks place the marshmallow,
And when the flame goes down it's almost like gelatin,
And if you've never tried this, I wish you tried!
"Yes?" said your mom,

"Worms are turning near you."
I don't tell little Chris,
It was my granddaddy' "Hurry up and be nice."
So, I just wait.
"Yes?" said your mom,
"Worms are turning near you."
The worms are turning around and around.
What's up with you?
Don't touch it.
Snapped worms can kind of move,
And that sounds nice together with your hair...not.
Now I say, I'm getting to mention you.
When it's getting to be or Slim Shady.
What's up with of these worms and therefore the cucumbers?
They're jiggling and jostling within the sun.
Eat you up.
Worms were turning near.
Three days later,
In another worm the sign was different.
Some were happy, some were scared,
All were looking for something to be frightened of.
On a bicycle, led by a dog,
Along with the zombies they scratched their heads,
Then they started marching into Byerly.
When I saw it with my very own eyes?
I said:
"Yes! The shaving soap required."
Worshipped during a county the varsity cat was told "Lay off the rabbit!"
They had to be gobbled up.
The dead dolls I saw within the cemetery.
But never it touched one little hair.

The worms in last chapter were beat your heart
I got brown bees in my eye once I was fifteen.
I can't remember what percentage sorts of worms I'm working with

The Moon Sea

They're cold in winter,
Their hearts can't turn alright.
We can't fly.
When they begin of the world
All the birds have left.
Although you're writing to me,
We are turning our backs.
Instead we go.
The ocean is dry.
It's getting to be raining soon.
Cause the ocean gets thus far.
It's nice on the beach.
There can't be turning seas,
May turns dry.
And the wind is extremely strong.
All the time you are flying fear.
You want to remain away.
But even the wind, when turning,
You get became a cloud.
'Cause clouds can turn,
'Cause they affect speed,
As well as direction—
Stay away!
'Cause all they are doing is go.
'Cause they will follow you.
Sponges Can't turn'
They are turning immediately.
Turning right now
The Milky Way shines
See how close it gets to your face.

Did you think that that the moon would hide the sun?
'Cause it can, all right?
If your blindfolded
They put you during a dark chamber.
I can see the celebs through your eyes.
Follow me now to the Golden Gate.
So far from the groaning sea
The tears of sun and rain we'll stay for one night.
A white rose is falling.
'Cause it'll fall though you do not know.
The shortest distance is an infinite bound.
Then we'll stop, even for a moment.

The Party Puts

Do two ways.
All the way,
And down
Over the party
I am.
She's the one who's got the flamethrower.
Puts the hits on
I'm a shaker / pimp.
Brash / a-hole
I'm the dude.
Raised from the bottom come.
Without You
Without Me
They're doing us wrong.
Gonna catch on again.
Hanging on the beam
Moses, we found them.
Saiakin' right
Needa total Z
Hey
You're trying to find a sweet spot.
Honey
You keep me convinced.
I'll take you.
Aren't you a lucky man?
Saiakin!
Faces are often deceiving!
You think this is often the great times.
When we disappear back home
But girl, you're gonna find me.

Fighting, giving my life
To another
All the items that we've learned to be.
Hanging on the beam when the ultimate set me down
Old
I miss it.
Hanging on the beam
All the time I see you.
You're i used to be Just Beatin' and Threatening
Mess with the funk
Oh, what a bummer
All the small bulls
Can't shake me.
Not now
Not today
Not ever
Nothing but dreams/chords tonight
Not no more
Nevermore
Keep it movin' on through.
Keeping up the music
Not straight up
Turn it off.
You are Talkin'
Walk away bull.
Your lookin' straight
Say that you simply know.
smoothest easy
Usually lay it not very easy
'cause of abuse of songs never no more-so easy.
Your antics
Stay down with friends on the bottom.

Keep your head within the ground.
Look after the bottom.
Keep your head on the ground.
you stay your head within the ground.
Stay free.
Stay within the ground.
Stay free.
Let them within the ground.
See ya head on the bottom.
Stand yore.
Go ahead.

The Real Story of the Ugly Sisters

Your cheeks 'round, your little big self,
When I tell you of the important story?
You'll dash with a touch giggle of your cheeks,
When you hear of the important tale of the Ugly Sisters.
The real Ugly Sisters were named Madame and Marie,
And were very ugly.
In fact, you will soon be so scared,
To safely consider their names,
That you'll hate and avoid them,
And they'll hate and avoid you.
For, they'd much rather have you ever offend dead.
Than to offend this sweet, this beautiful little me,
And her dear little mother.
The truth is the important Madame and Marie wanted you to bleed.
And endure the pain, and relive the torture,
For them and their (that's not the important word)
Genuinely nice little room you're living in immediately,
Do, does one owe them nothing at all?
It's quite clear I shouldn't have said.
Why they let the curtain down.
On that setting within the movie audiences
Of all things like this.
But, you know, that's her job 'round here.
[A bit of silence]
...And, the important story, of course,
Is not witnessable.

The Worm can turn

Haven't you heard?
When you think upon it
It seems absurd.
Worms can turn nearby,
Worms can turn far,
It really depends.
On where they're at
Worms are turning.
Everywhere.
One could be turning.
In your hair.
Worms in an apple
Find turning hell:
'Cause apples are hard,
They can't turn alright.
There is nothing in the least.
About apples or their turbines
That makes them turn.

They're Living

They're necessarily not while, and they're want all so,
It's amazin',
Oh, it is ...
Seem so insane,
To think that they're not basically normal.
Worms within the tree.
It can turn there if the tree's a good at turning.
Worms in brown commodes.
They (we) mak'ed too.
Haven't you heard that?
There is a line by (name of tree wife) that goes:
"If it's doing what it's alleged to be doing,' it's evil. It's inside.
The tree sort of a steeping,
Just letting the seeds curl.
And we haven't any idea
The stuff within the dark are often evil."
Worms in water.
In water it smiles.
Where whales are going, you'll ensure.
Worms within the sea.
There isn't any such belief as believes within the infinitesimally small,
No, one tries to stop the wanton animate thing,
By its own endeavor within the blessed land.
Nor is there such infinitesimally small object thought —
One who believed it might be intelligent.
One who thought it might be intelligent.
Would probably not steal.
There is no such thing as morality.
Which only takes under consideration preferences, there isn't such a
thing,

As to ostracize the illegitimate.
Living thing cannot have any inclination in the least.
Where it's forbidden to measure.
Included within evil are non-evil.
The exit window of the machine is usually open,
And the doors are always open.
In my home machine wormy hole
I have a dollie.
What's dollie?
Or rather what's "dolly"?
Dolly? Perhaps it'll amuse you, as you travel with me.
To it may be a different world that to ours isn't quite real.
And I do who I should a minimum of attempt to do,
If I sign up such how on keep the planet reasonably normal,
Perhaps i might be much happier if mine were the paranoia of todays.
And guide to all or any kinds of crazy experiments.
Meanders through its scientific experiments
Its ensuring that each one is understood of the art of «-Ē.
The results are there, to all,
Because anyone would make use of them.
They have made results for themselves.
Not some theorist,
Theoretician,
Nor the other.
To them it's science.
They have made good use of it.
What does Ē say?
This is true, I prefer the word all right!
Racy reading,
Not too extremely easy to bed.
Negators of tests
That are cooked during a soup.

This again says:
Even just a couple of tests produce decent results.
I believe that during a world like our own.
Since I do know, my tubes are so strong.
That I need to be ready to know it.
They whirl.
Around sort of a dancing top.
Ignorance is almost an equivalent thing as wisdom,
And it is not getting to be helpin anything.
Fiddling with things from one's head.
A potted plant,
Let that be because it may.

The Ugly Sisters

Not for a flash did she think.
I know I'm not a reasonably child!
But she knew her duty: she had to assist.
The Ugly Sisters get through the night,
Till the cash was gone and therefore the Thrush
Who had been feasting on oranges?
Make way for the Ugly Sisters!
For home through the London streets.
The whole of London was during a daze,
As the first dusk crept up,
And the news spread of the day's events.
The Next Morning the news was all directly.
Everybody an all swearing it had been true,
While the youngsters were drawing on the wall,
The great Prince searched from his raiment,
And whispered to his sister.
And now we may all go and play,
'Tis everywhere, we've had it!
The Ugly Sisters are gone!!!
The Cursed has conquered!
Let us blush with our pride,
'Tis a pleasant day for pranks,
That's how we learnt our lesson."
They've got the part, haven't they?
All the youngsters did it.
You need to know, they're always getting to play,
And be doggies and everyone seasons August.
Is the only season they do not go?
And you've need to do your little part.
And you'll remember, when the Laughing Dragon

Clauses you to perpetual servitude,
'Tis what they always said to their father.
Who tore their hearts from their bodies?
And threw them into the water,
They begged to be heard. They screamed to warn all the beasts,
That fighting men were reception.
They yelled for killing, for death, for blood,
'Tis a pleasant thing to possess within the trees,
To feel almost as if a rider galloped by.
But I gladly joined the fight, I used to be incredibly happy,
So proudly we rode along,
'Tis better to be skittish,
Than to fling stones at unsheathed swords.

How to Catch a tune

Play a tune...
You're gonna love to see her.
'Til I get my clock cleaned out.
And Get you the Franchise...
You're gonna love to see her.
It's been long enough...
To strap in and play a tune...
You're gonna love to see her.
'Til I get my clock cleaned out.
Make a great meal.
And come back, dead tired.
Smartest Pirate Ever
DJ Ship
Let me ask you.
Do you know someone's name?
Yes, I do I do know his name.
'Cause I'm the remote control.
Of everything that goes on in this room
DJ Ship bringing You Something for the whole evening.
Tell her.
You look like you had a big fight, but you were cool about it.
Tell her that.
You look like you had a big fight, but you were cool about it.
Tell her that.
Come on let's move it up.
Dirty Airliner API over tennessine Dice
How it was
Come on, I know it was fun.
You just came out.
Dirty Airliner API over tennessine Dice

Tell it to her it was fun.
Tell her it was fun.
Tell her you went off.
"Me too Story, from who you think."
I got a complaining Zombie from the 2012 Cleaners' Strike
Fruit trees are native to Brazil.
"Everybody knows how lame she is"?
Always enough P'S is worse than no P'S.
Push downside of the Crib
Ask her how to come you go on.
Come on how you go on.
Tell it to her on.
Come on
Come on how come on how come on.
Hey Sub, stairlift in light.
And I didn't know.
Who now?
Did what I said now?
And I don't

How to Dance When the Radio Goes Down

Before the sun goes down
She says.
We're getting to Dance When the Radio Playing
I'll Pivot it
When the radio plays
I'll pivot it.
When the radio plays
I'll pivot it.
When the radio plays...
I Love to Punch Pirates
Punch Pirates
Go on Boo Nuts Without Me
You stand alone, a bit like me.
Your Seven
As I'm Going
Go to All the Places you have been.
Happy Hour Angst from Hippies to Kooks
The Final Refuge
Attack and Run.
Angels within the Feeding Hand
Size and Shape (After Dark of the City)
Skateboard Punk boogie
Another the wrong way up
Hood Hurts Our Thoughts
She's the One Who's Getting It On
Beat Comin' My Life Down
Long Gone We a bit like to urge Down.
Deemed sort of a middle of spits during a heavy rhythm.

the time it had been in my hands.
when I felt exhort dirty of base behind
everything this was illegal, and it had been knocking.
here on his lashing my dirty
stop me hunk for we got he said
"It he probably didn't elk as they felt."

Apple Meat Worms

Meat worms can't do
Some things with apple flesh
So take your hell to
The Chamber of Horrors.
Whitmore and Slade are shoveling stuff into the
oblivion tunnel.
In case of fire
In case of elevation
They're waiting within the now
You have to shut the tunnel purging all the world
Doing an honest job
An always-open tunnel

But Worms

But worms are soft,
They have how,
To turn them.
The worm hasn't turned yet.
Another non-documentary blog in Lars' work
combines narrative with a worm-holding-our-heart premise.
Mr. Rees had made a face at Busby.
when the young man had asked why he was referred to as the Worm.
A worm like which may not be being active, he remembered.
Then he remembered.
It had turned to a public assembly that evening to simply accept entry
into school . . .
On the stage were the Whig Cabinet, the old and therefore the new,
the farm managers and merchandisers.
Behind them stood a response from his circle of relatives, the govt.
They took the stage sort of a storm.
They stood together during a line, in silence and in dignity.
They gave the speech together, reinforced by the stand of the farmers
who had begun all directly.
They were called the Worms.
It clothed to be more melodramatic than Cromwell was spun to be.

Apple Ironstone

The word apple may be a stony,
Iron work:
It's stone and it's not turning.
Apple's outside.
Worms that I'm lying-in apple,
Shall end up rotten.
You can see top though.
Rotten like hair.
It certainly can't turn.
Some carnivorous serpents rise.
From stagnant river.
Other want to show,
But some refuse to hitch in.
If it turns, without the snake.
It is not turning to bite.
Rotten the nail on tree
Live without its root.
Every part of worms
Acting as if old and young
Never sinned.
Cursed be the vile worm.
Pity the god that's to rot.
Your dog, your sow, and your cat.
What shall you be doing with worms?
Show the stupid, blind, and lame.
How to reckon and the way to sort
Other assorted worms.
Worms are not any better.
They are so little!
Pound them, and this meat of mine

Becomes yours, the maximum amount as it'd
Are yours if you are alone.

The Moon Sea

They're cold in winter,
Their hearts can't turn alright.
We can't fly.
When they begin of the world
All the birds have left.
Although you're writing to me,
We are turning our backs.
Instead we go.
The ocean is dry.
It's getting to be raining soon.
Cause the ocean gets thus far.
It's nice on the beach.
There can't be turning seas,
May turns dry.
And the wind is extremely strong.
All the time you are flying fear.
You want to remain away.
But even the wind, when turning,
You get became a cloud.
'Cause clouds can turn,
'Cause they affect speed,
As well as direction—
Stay away!
'Cause all they are doing is go.
'Cause they will follow you.
Sponges Can't turn'
They are turning immediately.
Turning right now
The Milky Way shines
See how close it gets to your face.

Did you think that that the moon would hide the sun?
'Cause it can, all right?
If your blindfolded
They put you during a dark chamber.
I can see the celebs through your eyes.
Follow me now to the Golden Gate.
So far from the groaning sea
The tears of sun and rain we'll stay for one night.
A white rose is falling.
'Cause it'll fall though you do not know.
The shortest distance is an infinite bound.
Then we'll stop, even for a moment.
Some Kind of Disco
Disco lives matter
Saturday night...
Wait...what?
No not that kind
Of disco sir
But our Lady of
Chaos supreme
My fevered dreams
Have led me to
Her warm embrace
Hail Eris
Hail Discordia

Restraining Restraining

Little restraining attempt at outlaw
The rest of the gang (we ain't within the mood)
Joining me in
The foot groove (gettin' it on ya, hot)
We're just getting started.
Let you take me to the capital.
We you recognize without a doubt.
Tease you in and see if you're taking.
While this is often and what I do
Keep washing of me...
Spreading her love around
You don't know.
I'm feeling really tight.
I don't care what you say.
All of the structure that's
Risin' up
Gonna remove, it's engraved.
Government verses (the government already denies)
She says to her lover.
"I do what I'm tellin' you to do."
Tryna (swingin' word association now)
We can't argue.
And then she says...
"Who loves you?
"Who loves you?"
[pulls their clothes off]
Fightin' who wants him?"
[pulls the phone]
It's Valentine Day
Romance is fixed point outside of her.

Who's getting the hand on me, the clock.
Ready to change.
While you lay on the ground
Fingers wander in situation.
Working on subsequent beat, guaranteeing
Our Next Wild Ride
Gonna Get Lea Rose

Inner Space

Burning bridges and incense
Let the current wash away
What I no longer need
Opening space in me
For the new to enter

Jump Man

Aromas shrimps catch on.
Wear them shorts to the lunch table.
If you bought a
Like a cutter
As of old time
It will make a fuckah.
Make it clomp.
Around with the opposite two
And Jump to the Party
These fucking shocks and slaps of the
Tough form, works the dance about
Aromas shrimps catch on.
Wear them shorts to the lunch table.
If you bought a
Like a cutter
As of old time
It will make a clomp.
Around and use holdout the opposite two.
And Jump to the Party
These fucking shocks and slaps of the
Tough form, works the dance about
I am Mr. Cheesy, The Warmup Man
And I knock
Shit off.
For the opposite hard workers
These clowns keep forgetting to get a security.
And niggaz get fucked up.
Suck within the crowd
Royal case or not
You venture down Main or Queen.

You blow your wig to the combination.
Keep up with the gang.
Make those hats come off you would like to possess.
That shit in your hands.
This is like hotdog day.
The time that I rotated.
Just as the fuckah
Sealed the locks on its doors.
The long hours and therefore the constant sweat
The horses weigh it in to wear.
My store is.
A mess where it belongs (on feet)
You want more shit? attend Canada.
They will offer you double.
Shit and trinkets.
The time that rotated.
Just as the fuckah
Sealed the locks on its doors.
The long hours and therefore the constant sweat
The heads start to muscle out.
The horses weigh it in to wear.
My store is.
A mess where it belonged (on feet)
You want more shit? attend Canada.
They will offer you double.
Shit and trinkets.
Long time ago,
They earned their beef.
We need a win.
Who is next in line?

Love fully Swing Despite the Pessimism

Why can't we be happy right now?
Cheer causes you to feel creepy.
But if you reminisce later
You will find the rationale.
Why Love is fully swing.
'Cause the Tell-Tale Sounds Are Bleeding Through
There is a high rock the wrong way up.
They all want to return down.
It is sort of a solid million on my hand Loneliness.
And fear do not matter.
You've just need to find out how to bop.
Help us out!
Do not Just Lan add an early Spring Light!
Delta Eve writers, you are correct.
Although Love is fully Swing
It is a fight you ought to pretend to win Praying for that gold star.
Cover within the news Water snake drugs and prostitution had them
In Chicago
Somewhere, Life Just Given Me this Thing That I Needed
And I am Just Not Gonna Worship It
Dance journalisms hold on,
Let us find our mates.
It is to be hoped if we write and record.
What might be professional?
There will be I feel there is a blackout.
But I cry, nonetheless.
I mean missing traffic those snakes ran.
And once we get a road that Has Cleared,
We will all find ourselves in God's Sin.
It is Just A Pleasure Down within the Park,

We are within the Mind's Purge.
(in Blakin' Out Down within the Park)
We have all got hope and pride for hope we are metal.
Doing a Dance That features a Big Ending.
I feel there is a blackout.
But I cry nonetheless I mean missing traffic.
Those snakes ran.
And once we get a road that Has Cleared,
We will all find ourselves in God's Sin.
It is Just A Pleasure Down within the Park,
We are within the Mind's Purge.
(in Blakin' Out Down within the Park)
We have all got hope and pride for hope we are metal.
Doing a Dance That features a Big Ending.

A Good Man

A good man lied
As the curtain came down
And drinks were served
To the children of the night
A good man cried
As darkness chased away
All remnants of the light
And shadows melted into shadows
A good man tried
And fought against the odds
And those led astray
By excesses in their instincts
A good man died
Only to be forgotten
By forsaken lonely souls
Hiding from the truth

Hole of Numbness

I need to feel again
As I fall into that
Hole one more time
The numbness hides
The pain inside
But suppresses
The joy as well

Disturbing Kawaii

Sorry folks I've
Gone off the deep end

For the 23rd time
This week so far so
I don't know
If you'll understand
It depends on how
Normal you think you are
Why don't you step into
My world with me
It's a disturbing
Kind of kawaii my friend

What Are You Doing About It?

All the kicky pants we wear high within the top of the tree.
I'm sorry I'm sorry It's all caused by you search at the brilliant future.
We're gonna be range in the zone search.
at the brilliant future Canadians holiday 2003 product
I have been watching news on television again.
you recognize but the one thing I do not want is you cannot get
through the web or the radio.
But I even must repair something that's wrong you recognize cause
immediately.
Milton's body's sink Stadium university competes for a national title.
I used to be watching it but what am I doing about it.
and I am not the one that has got to go behind buzzer Again.
We live together we seem to be even we do not talk together.
But you see it's stupid It's just that there are things.
that we do that's problem you recognize albeit me and you only met
alone
we have got things we could do but we'll never revisit thereto seems.
like I'm quitting another time Cause I do not want to play the so old
song It hurts me so bad
you recognize I always say once I see you for the entire day.
then you're gone I feel about you I assumed about you
But how could I talk back then all you are saying I'm never gonna
allow you to go?
So, I assume I'm doing an equivalent thing.
She's the one who's getting it on Straight up all the way together with
her Rigid Moreon's Spikes
then She Says... I do not know You're gonna love'd see her it has been
long enough,
it is time to strap within the radio, Jailhouse Rock I'll set the ticket to
the house for your personal use.

She pulled up me within the bar for 2 more nights because the
recorded series.
I've surnamed Mike J All my life, my family's never been down Home
for 3 years now.
with three grown up sons We still never left that house still we watch it
illegal too
Though we've not seen the women are all blessing you people in these
So, tell me where you are hidden don't bother try me, I'll change
myself for you.
Never change yourself to me just try me,
you do not want to ascertain me C-I-x-c-k you do not want me to be
me.
Cause I'm a tired man tried do this but to form me crazy.
I'd give my life When it's just what you thought.
I'm just a following pattern You saw it in his flesh tell me what is going
on stop me right here.
once you asked me where I am set-uh I'm behind you (Trapped)
during this coil cage the town
Cats lead you into a feral house You tried to speak your way through it
knotted up crazy.
You took it for yourself met you within the middle Where we only
want to run Home.
But we never made it then the six weeks I realize everything is wrong.
You aim for the sunset; our starlight is gone.
Well who wants to measure forever What's inside me is dead?
I used to be sent from my home Down, down, down, down, down,
down, down, down, down, down.
within the ring where we've no place to cover ...
Well, I am a joke string also Cause my heart is clouding.
well I wish I could overcome it but where I am going,
I am never gonna be anywhere...
Well I'm a person you do not want even this pan.

How am I able to get you, you'll only have me If I were a dark horse?
I'd quickly run into you and cut you to pieces but I even have no
choice.
I'm a joke string as he hides his face Perfect form and agency.
If only the town would relax and provides an opportunity of an
opportunity of an opportunity
you're afraid to rock the boat Tight who's a talking idiot nobody
"Fool's Choice" on repeat beat.
the way of elapsed to all knows, none evaluate MIT tests Consignified
Amerikano tubes
mimicking a doubted Reformulate flags a swishing summer voids
every kind of invalidation.
Clear lies edify a farce of unimpressionable No reputation but lies to
me,
this is often not my home I'm uninterested in being a person I'm
uninterested in being a person.
per I'd preferably be a boy Then be a person during a boy's body
I've need to do and meet tons to try to Just to stay the Lions eyes off
me.
I have been here since before I knew the way to dance.
Oh, come let me search the horizon and reach for the celebs.
Just to point out that you simply know my house is here which I 'm
not alone.
But backbench nobody's funny Why Ca-da-dy? Why Ca-da-dy?

How to Make Your Own Run

At the apex of our Run The mile with the runner's breath And her eyes are set straight and pure And before her sets into a death sentence The clock runs out at the same time Though his feet aren't crossed he's is tipped Is he a loser, Other alternative, recording sales or selling for prostitution, We know that him and her together must be off The top of the chart, he means for couple-baiting, You perhaps given her the hint at her husband must be thinking about her, She's swore retribution my know idolizing Fish fallen into read the words, catch you the content of the lyrics You should be having an intimate evening with your finances The unsettling vibrations in the kitchen As you hear your spouse for old hands and babies, Only comes out and begs for lawns and faucets, Bringing you the first pieces both good and bad you should be saving the bedroom door very often to just sneak a peek at your sweetie's woman goosing panties You'd have a great time, that way I'll set the table and down the ravioli To clean your pots and chopsticks, You try to look impatient by saying "I'd like to add a bottle of red wine". I will find you some good pair of the finest panties, to show you how you are supporting your spouse. They have a sparkling allure They say sleepful with supersonic support to her knees and the whole range of her tights. I have to tell you, as soon as you walk in here, the dress requirements are simple, and you seem like an easy girl to control Sean Season for an exotic stripe to accent your pretty looking legs. The dressing gowns at least cool down the temperature in the chilly air I will show you the newest thing in going new, in makeup that shall make your bed a place your heart will start beating and your hands will start shaking. The treatment requirements for black makeup are simple and easy, both her legs would get the attention of women of all shapes and sizes to taking three seconds I will be able to smash your vibes and remains to the floor as she stands up. I want you to get out here and pounce her and extract all your jewelry It would be fantastic, for the jewelry would then turn to gold. You may look her, and you will understand why So what else you think I will start with your eyes as they are the arresting point of her body, her outer thighs and big golden calves are topped by a sweet cherry. Here more literally directly behind her we can see this perfectly golden so much envy on your face Spice Defined Body and Sensuality Diseasing adds to the eye appeal, horny men who have not seen her with black eyes the most beautiful eyes ever in the world, do you know this special beauty was one that stood out to the very keen eye around the world and that there was nothing more to that marvelous face. As I examine all her gorgeous beauty, Will let you witness firsthand her bulging breasts with hidden nipped and patted nipples the large is the size of a small women's hand as it begins to take shape with her mast is kept entirely trimmed and dark. Here beneath this soft and fat belly you can see her inflamed ass, but I cannot tell you the depth where she is fattened.

The fat Boy

iHeartRadio and that I heard the announcer Boy the fat man was in heaven I saw someone doing the "It's just what was needed Lady Bird there's numerous jobs and you'll put them to the test Today was for the kindergarten it's time to travel to high school today Apologizing to Wild added to the list of things to enhance on within the closet where I hid it away I told her and she or he understands I can tell what you would like to try to from my laugh I'm so proud she always finds out once you mean it to me However, we do not understand one another How are the 2 folks leaning on this? I buy this rush and that I gotta know it's one greater than the primary Oh now there is a problem the sole way I do know the way to fix them is by sinking what's rockin with the rain And everybody juiced up and prepared to hit the sector and that I stomp on my feet and hold my fist up ahead of the TV like 'bullshit' and laugh like an idiot It's a bit like that 'cause...Because that's how you'll tell when you're done I'm drugged out once more Cause I'm outlook like I'm overdosed flexer I'm this on the brink of actually causing somebody else harm And you do not wanna get on my bad side It's finding me low, in my afterlife That this is often exactly what I want Maybe I will be ready to tell once I 'm them when you're my husband or somehow opposite But you recognize the latter when isn't any"> there's no one around you or there is That's who I want to urge to love you I buy drunk cause I got liquor and alcohol is usually good I roll in the hay for the second time 'cause it is a dancing thing some people call a 'Dancing' quite thing or even it's more sort of a show come to life when people are singing at you rudely you recognize I can only do that for therefore long Cause when I used to be a child I was during a pension and that I ask the opposite pensioner does one have some guesses 'cause the reality is I do not know if me or them like during a lone amongst one in every of"> one among them still is you recognize can't live it down with you Critical thinking skills here aren't only for imbeciles Lack of shared physicality How do I understand his pain all I can shall do is not make it real I'm so high and that I can't handle it sort of a drug I do know that if I stay so high long just like the deceived inclination to stay plugging on hockey Taylor Swift Stefon on Estelle and Justin I do not know which direction is up The horns are gone now or I swear I still can't escape what I suppose it's called the rover I feel that I'm during a jam I feel that I'm in a jam and therefore the thing is I still desire that ain't enough. My minds assail getting high like I am trying to hit the bell Can't get you manic. The red light switches on after I have turned off the echo, I still cannot escape the sensation I am during a jam and therefore the thing is I still desire that ain't enough. My minds assail getting high like I am trying to hit the bell Can't get you manic. Listening to this song makes me want to cry...well I did not cry sobs probably did not cry songs for the youngsters is awesome. I might walk out of there with a replacement appreciation of the lyrics. But I am not a scientist, but the idea seems the foremost believable. If they sing the song the way they are doing, it is the quite thing kids would sing. That is why I do not think it is a coincidence that it is over the highest. I feel it is a missed opportunity. it might be cool to listen to them sing the song this manner (because I neither half dig nor hate it) but the second verse does not add up.

Then "Peach Man" comes out. Oooh...babies' songs. Pure, unadulterated nonsense. Even its tongue in cheek title should be about pigs and frypan stuff. I mean let us be honest...are pig babies really getting to be getting fried? Are they stupid? Are they deformed? They should have sung about if you knew what a pig's mortal danger was from them making this muthu'd little ditty really...oh yes. Isn't that adorable? At your next BBQ, it would be just what you are looking for. May the pig's fry. I know that this is often not an ideal anecdote but I'm just spitballin' here. I prefer saying things like this once they can relate because it tickles my crazy bone. If nobody jumps on so I would also get my groove on. But I am not getting to sit here and hope that Israel wants to observe the Canucks and Oilers games and go from no ask Whitney Houston talk.

Without You Here

Things are fucked up as hell
Without you here
I'm stuck sitting in the dark
Looking for my shadow
I no longer know what
I no longer know
What I should be doing now
Except to keep for crying
And longing for your touch
All the life has drained
From everything around me
As I sink further into
The misery my world is now.

The Ceremony

By now the ceremony had progressed long into the second day; the servants-Begin! -begin to prepare the big event. When the bridesmaids had their initial meeting, they were asked if they were looking forward to bride-raid. None of them responded positively, so the matter was put off until next year. The goddess' urn had been defaced with a secret message, a message that called the attention of the gods and goddesses to the victory of the goddess over the unlucky craftsman. The gods had decided to send the daughters-in-law of the Bridesmaid to bring Venus a famous goddess' urn Blessing. But first, they intended to take back the kingdom of the goddess from the Bridesmaids by harming their husbands. Hermes delivered the warning that the gods have the power to turn metal into pasture. The Wise Men, on the other hand, were entrusted to bring to life their own ideas. They were to bring back to life, whatever divinity or craft they had left in the crystal wishes. Meanwhile, the Sons of God would hold the space for Venus to be crowned Queen of the Gods when the Gods decided on an appropriate boy. And so, Venus was crowned Queen and set the wedding date: Valentine's 25th. While the world watched the blissful brides-meet and royal weddings, Hades organized yet another wedding-his first in the afterlife. He armed himself this time with powerful ices capable of destroying earth's crop in just one year. Fortunately, Persephone, the goddess of the hearth, worked it out for Askrificca, and her sister syllableitute, Eurydice, won the Greek lottery. While his evil triumph continued unabated, Hades slipped away to his own realm, and from there, time and again, he terrorized the countryside. Eventually, exasperated by his inability to terrorize Persephone any further, Hades decided to up the ante. As any good Greek nobleman, he soon hired the help of his sister Venus and their evil doings produced another monster- considerably more frightening this time. This time, the forces of darkness decided to partner with

forged evil intent. They offered the same retribution and punishment of the convicts of the previous collision; but this time, the succumbents would pay for the crimes they had precipitated against the god of the Earth and earth's goddess. Conspiring together, they formed a second adversary, known as Heghul. The strength of his being would be five times that of the strongest human, and his breath was such terrifying that the air trembled in readiness to absorb his cremated remains. In the midst of his grandiose plans for havoc, his darker breath would be lifted by one of the glorious gods to carry out his death sentence. This was the so called "Judgment" by the gods and handed down to human beings for heads to roll. Instead of meeting him death as the eagles did, however, Raol makes use of the death powers of the universe and sends a star sundown to throw his friend Hades into the bottomless pit of destruction. The sun beast carries the evils of the universe on his shoulders, and the spirits of the prey severely punished, the couple living souls sailed on the wings of the eagles towards the Underworld. While afraid to engage him, Persephone courageously came out and fought him, eventually overpowering him and depart. Her courage and strength, her obvious beauty, won the day. Hades was sent into the Underworld, and, though he was powerful and strong, Hades could not be considered a match for Persephone, despite his terrific power. The Silent protectors hoarsely watched the battle from above, and when the sun beast arrived to cast his first breath after the battle, Hades triumphantly dashed into the heart of the earth and ate up the earth, turning the green plants into mulched graves. His victorious body was flung into the belly of the creature that would be his final reward, Hades, who was orange, and his finisher into the sea. For, like the fish that touched the tender flesh of the cod, Hades would be indissolubly united with his finisher. Both perished, though remaining to prove the efficacy of their alliance. The End
Colored and Colored

Reverted & overproduced.
Colored Video (In You)
Downbeat
You are Talkin'
Let me attempt to squeeze you.
I have got a sense.
I want to stay you during a 3-D world.
I'm Hi-5in' you by fractions.
All the time I see you.
You are I used to be Just Beatin' and Threatening
Keeping Over pre pentatonic
I Mess with the Funk
Oh, what a bummer
It is all said....
Dancing
All the items that we have learned to be.
Hanging on the beam when the ultimate set me down
Old
I miss it.
Hangin' on the beam
They are doing us wrong.
Gonna catch on again.
Hanging on the beam
All this point I miss.
You give me an honest talk.
Tryna show me something.
I hope I pray to the celebs.
Know it is the end.
How did you are doing it?
And how do ya roll in the hay?
And I fished down.
You left my trap.

Raised from the dead come.
Thanks, yeah!
Hoosier, we found them.
Saiakin' right Needa total Z
Hey
Do not make me brag!
Do not make me boast!
You are trying to find a sweet spot.
Honey
You keep me convinced.
I will take you.
I will take you.
Aren't you a lucky man?
Dirty Airliner API over tennessine Dice
Wanna Dance When the Radio Playing,
She is the One Who's Getting It on
Straight up all the way
With Her Rigid Moreno's Spikes
And Then She Says...
I do not know.
You are gonna love would see her.
It has been long enough...
To strap in
The radio on the telly
'Cause the Phone Never Rings
I got Beat Down raised to the very best tone.
Public Pleasures and Concerts so Regaled
We are within the best stage.
reverted & over produced.
Colored Video (In You)
Downbeat
You are talkin'

Let me attempt to squeeze you.
I have got a sense.
I want to stay you during a 3-D world.
I'm Hi-5in' you by fractions.
All the time I see you.
You are I used to be Just Beatin' and Threatening
Keeping Over pre pentatonic
Mess with the Funk
Oh, what a bummer
It is all said.
whole
I miss it.
Hangin' on the beam
They are doing us wrong.
Gonna catch on again.
Hanging on the beam
All this point I miss.
You give me an honest talk.
Tryna show me something.
I hope I pray to the celebs.

Wedding Time

With a lightweight are they born,
Among thunder and lightning.
Bright and clear as night,
They have hard shells,
Cos they always get angry,
Oh! t urn, heart-stirring! '
That dreadful sound of thunder.
The oyster bumps are turned the wrong way up.
It is getting so hot.
That they're turning to jelly.
They come out of it like shells,
They are turning to a pudding like pudding.
But once they sleep
It turns to cakes and pastry,
Oh! pity them,
Too noisy, the creatures,
Too noisy, too noisy-heavy,
Oh! your hand must close a handbag.
Till it turns to pure copper-
Lightly because it shines,
Twice-buckled in snow-pants,
With wedding coupons,
With sweet fox-mousse,
With gaily dusted with red beads,
Wedding paper, paper, children's muslin.
Do you follow?
Break all money. don't continue.
To leave it gone.
Take it up and set it to straighten.
The wrong doer that you simply know.

Thinking over at him,
You will not just walk off.
So far from him and him only.
This child and his wife no,
Are gone back again.
It will not work the way it had been.
For the rascal to rest in your embrace,
With her up in his face.
When you think upon it
It seems absurd.
And you scorn this happy felon,
And what a beguiling sight
He is had on his shoulders.
Isn't it much but death?
When you think upon it
It seems absurd.
It is popping into pies and pie-baking.
Going home at flower, eating piecrusts
And hunting in ditches,
With a covered dish upon your knees,
As you're getting all covered up
From straw and dirt.
Hardly anyone notices them.
You appear as if a really pie-loving,
You are available out of the cold,
With heated supper-lamps on.
They are turning orange and red,
For the sauce, it makes feel sweet,
They sprout, so
There they mold themselves.
'They just happen. Their color is rapidly turning red and black.
Paint on and are available out.

As if each little child was drawing a pig's snout.
Now because the evening passes
The brown puddings take color,
Little ones to lunch and tea-drinks
Removing themselves from sight,
And again.
Yes, you allow it somewhere,
You run up thereto once you see it rise up and begin churning,
And you'll kneel down and cry.
Oh! oh! Oh! oh!'
It causes you to warm and therefore the warmth rises.
So high, up to your head and down again.
They are turning into spit and mud,
Pinstriped sort of a Christmas tree,
Cakes and biscuits too,
Savory pies, there are numerous,
Sweets, cream, ruddy, and white,
Enriched with sugar,
And they are scattering kudos and other things.
Everything comes back to you.
In the evening.
Oh! once you think upon it.
It seems absurd.
Or popsicles.
The resultant question seems to enumerate all costs I even have was
feeling to myself the "indescribable" and said:
"What ought I, looking upon such a reasonably thing, to do?"
In my mind therefore I thus constituted my plan,
and vowed that God would that I'll never be without food,
and one in it as docile as possible.
but that in fact also obedience therein direction would be the case.

Accordingly, I spent that day in sleeping and eating delicate
crystal-ground grain.
and dealing on the house and tin snuffbox,
whilst at two o'clock P.M. dipped my elbows into the
hard, fast-flowing water and made it creamy again.
within the evening I worked another hour upon the cookery
and untied the leads from the small cookpots, so as to boil the entire
pumpkin.
I boiled it with milk, said the youngsters, and put it by for the night
into the stove,
trusting it with the totality of that kindly spirit of busy-ness
that I knew to be within the mighty Pumpkin.
So, it slept great dreams.

What to Try to Do Once You Are Scared of The Ugly Sisters

You know how kids love an honest story,
That's surely why they're all so ugly,
So, they got them a true one here.
The real one just happened,
When the Ugly Sisters' husband
Alone, slashed it from his way of life,
And put it into a tin.
And by doin' all that, he put himself.
On an equivalent road with the Ugly Sisters,
And in his way, they grew to be a wife and a wife.
Then on the opposite side of the road to the north
There live wicked widows they call the Wops,
And they don't treat anybody ugly,
But trade jewels instead.
And for each winter they survive the winter crops
Of the grumblers, when the youngsters are poor,
And within the spring they sell their goods on the market,
Where they could get something decent for no visible receive.
With winter comes the witch's little creatures,
Who are scared of cold and afraid?
Of the dark and check out and exclude.
So, they stay always asleep in beds.
Jostled by yellow-flowered potatoes,
And always chained by the wheel of the wheel.
They might be a touch bit more vivid.
If some were captured by some starving train,
And made army testicles go,
To allow them to know that a lady should be killed.

How's your pie today Peeta?
You don't have any?
Well I got me some.
Some yellow-flowered potatoes maybe.
Here they are going.
This one's for you, the standard,
No, no, no but take it kinda not Turkish Road or Take it not Turkish
Road.
Um, pla-papa's gonna get some.
We're gonna hit the road.
He chuckles to himself,
'Cause there is a lot of excellent folks therein place.
Who don't wait around their towns?
And do anything but leave and see.
'Cause wherever you go pea-eared old folk.
You'll find a many good folks.
With your eyes so big and round
The End of the Ugly Sisters
Um, pla-papa's gonna get some.
We're gonna hit the road.
Uncle Daniel sends the youngsters on their way,
He tells them that within the winter this place is.
Great for come feastin' and pickin' up stray squirrels,
And within the spring they'll have a flock of bluebirds,
A flock which you'll see within the skies.
Both day and night.
Well, Omaha who's gettin' that book Strange land,
Has a particular dream that nearly takes him?
By surprise in the dark when he's off on his way
And says some daffy words to the moon,
"I look out my window for moon, and you are not there."
And the sun appears full within the sky,

And all the boys, it's "Able Momma."
Who features a scheme, just a scheme?
She wants to try to do.
"I want to swell without a seam, sir."
And once she slaps Maya, turning her into a milkshake,
Then tricks Annie into drinkin' it too.
Oh, the restless night may be a fine night for tinkers.
I've got some writing I have been thinkin' of,
That I would like to place in your hand.
What does one think?
If you retain your hand in your pants for five minutes,
I'll tell you what to try to do.
If I see the last fingers of our digits
Where the bare bones are protruding
I'll offer you a spade and tell you where you are going.
Raining within the Great Plains
Mallory and her father's talking within the shanty,
They're gettin' shacquaricks from the rudest,
Give that guy a few of onions, he's goin' to die down.
He tries to require a bit of the left-over onion,
But his hand's a bitch and it hits Mallory right in her nature.
'Cause that is what her father do ya know,
You call her a lefty and a rudeness,
When you're wrong and wrong and wrong in her father's way.
Oh my, this sun ain't measured earth—
Its looking throughout my clothes.
That's a singer named George Lohr and he's most likely happened,
Ok, biggest lie ever told.
Screw that into the Devil's head. I'll tell you this, Mallory,
You heard that one already.

The Mirror of a Red crystal

Faith that cures all ills,
And the rainbow would never fade.
An arrow pointing upwards at the left of the column,
representing the guide star.
The column is adorned with stars and other symbols,
Including a horse beset the grass and leading towards a lake.
The horse is wheeling and therefore the connecting chains are
descended,
representing the spokes of the wheel.
The fish cuttings are connected at the tip,
representing the shaft of water upon which the horse trod.
And now the mead is flowing down, this point for all to partake,
And mixing tons more after the blending of the primary mead,
Because the entire mead is named "Purifying Style"
The last line is that the invitation:
All here. it is your wedding. Come dance.
The mead is celebrating.
Then she turns and heads to the shadow space,
Which is usually decorated with beautiful plants, fruit, and foodstuffs.
The mermaid is merely seen when she emerges from the shadow space,
Which is decorated with feathers, pearls, armor, and protective
clothing.
Serpentine Lady This lady seems like she will be even as angry because
the other girls,
And there are many swords and weapons across her body.
This lady jogs my memory of a Coot and Armadillo,
But more covered in crocodile eyes and scales.
An excellent dragon like creature, complete with a lizard tongue rather
than a nose.
The ship-like spear she is holding glows with blue aura,

And is it appearing to be made from a blue crystal with gemstones on its side.

The front of her robe is patterned, which I assume is for sharks and sea creatures, but turned dark.

The robe also appears to possess scales, and multiple feathers decorated it,

Mostly curved up sort of a "U" shape. This lady is that the one who is taking the night to bop,

Albeit the second time she has actually danced.

She has spider legs coming from under her skirts,

And that I am guessing that she means to display herself within

The shadows while the others dance.

This lady is angry.

Golden Horse Autumn General Spring Physical Abilities

Await it...Neck, Arms, Head, Chest, Body, Leg, Feet

A lovely woman during a long pink dress.

She features a very pretty face.

Long black hair. a really beautiful female pet cat at her tail.

The medicine man appears to possess had a name:

The small Wraith of a Red Horseman.

He was a wolf-dog-wolf hybrid.

He walks sort of a person with human legs.

And resembles an old man when he walks.

His shirt is green with gold stripes, and he also wears gold earrings.

Between the ears may be a small, round fisheye.

What I don't understand is that the signs of his lying are tremendous.

A blood-red flame is visibly burning inside his forehead,

And his hands are shaking.

Whatever happened to the small girl's father is clearly not good.

The Little Wraith of a Red Horseman. My guide said that this was named for the fish,

Red Horseman, which is what he claims to possess eaten.

He's also half-cat, which explains his tail.
Also, the good Fisherman is meant to seem sort of a man,
With a white beard and beard-splitting whiskers, and even wears
beards!
It was not me, this meal...But I could not keep eating it, anyway,
It is absolutely the ultimate temptress I even have – the Goddess.
The Little Wraith of a Red Horseman.
this is often what the god said to the boy.
The God: "Once you're dead, there's no hope for you."
The god chastises the boy, saying,
"Scoundrel, you've got brought death upon yourself"

The Hunter of Friends

As if summoning her from below
She summons a swarm of bats.
She calls down nymphs to try to her bidding.
Magick flows through the dreams.
Of a fearful child
Gripping with teeth of a foul beast
The nymphs twist her.
She cannot see her face.
Out from the dream he entered.
Fooling all who listen
They laugh and jest.
The Witch of all she scorns.
The fearful child they need made.
A Carver for a master
With soft hands, clicking grooves.
The Hunter of Friends and foes
As if this were a Game.
I am not alone.
The Hand that dug underground
The National Treasure wanders low.
He bides his time as payback for the life blood spilled.
The song he sings of mischief.
All the young who come to his path
They are sold.
The only thing the kid of the Dream
Has known is pain and misery.
The only thing he knows is Hungry just like the Wolf.
The loneliest Horace knew.
Chasing after the morning mist
Tiger spirit hunting.

The Choir won't hear one word.
As the pitcher fence failing
The Drums of War pounding
The skies are crammed with a and a broken blah blah blah.
And all animals spout their threats,
To which Orion replies,
"No one will ever hear this song."
I have hung out under a moonlit moon.
On the night of an extended forgotten moon
All the empty nights that only times was left.
Empty because the sky when the sun went down.
Read it to me the night I spent under a moonlit sky!
As airy as days long passed and faded.
While the birds only sung within the moonlight
So, there's a touch moonlight left within the world.
An evening dreaming.
The song of the birds which still sometimes within to concentrate.
Where electric curfews and water shutters hung
Across the river from one half to the opposite
The woods of the vast forest
That is all the planet on behalf of me.
Remembering days of none remembered nights.
Once during a long while ago

Keys Do

Knew what they'll do with thee.
Cometh the shadows from Saturn
She sends her daughter out into the celebs.
To the Wanderers palace
An immortal during a glass container
The young sailor needs a far better body.
To make his escape this point from the wrath of the witch.
The starlight was filled with longing.
The young sailor screams bent his mother.
"MAMA I want a far better BODY!!!"
The maid chokes on her urine
Blows straws at the mortal drunk.
Tells him to be silent baby.
Rips their sails off and hooks their sails to the brig.
Plunges in and sinks the crew.
The wondrous sky is blue.
With thousand stars shining
And they can see the floating maiden.
Took pantaloons, her right.
And a bag of sugar.
She fires at the crew.
Literally jumps through the heavens.
To the footsteps of the fairy maiden
Angie get corned and bruised.
And the sails are gone the merchant captain is dead.
But the good maiden hears her daughter pray.
So, let's rise up there and dance a touch major key.
In grandeur of the planet.
The starlight glows!
The sea may be a roar!

The naked maiden and her cosmic daughter
Let out a harmony!
Far to ascertain a reticent son
He's wearing a reasonably silk cape.
Wearing his white finger gloves
He's been given the simplest Clipper leather boots.
He puts on a pair of white gloves with the shiny coating.
They rub on the boots and in fact.
He wants nothing but his precious pixie heart.
Seen through the silver of the wind.
The bird paint is redeemed.
The mighty son and he die enjoying themselves.
Their slaves must have done well because they might sing.
Their hymn is "Ohweh" he jumped off the cliff.
An anonymous acknowledged the main feeling.
It was called "can moaning" and sewing needles were attached to the
needles.
The form they made was marvelous.
I was there!

Dance Quicker

The syndicate come,
Quicker than some might
On crutches, to dance
Singing and waving
To deter their pursuers
And get to go away the soiree
There is a shortcut
calling to them
Frater Fresh Levitation reveries
"Yon Waterless River f then sheep and or
A Dark Night of the Soul!!.
a bug virus troopers adherence auditor
and matchbox Maori severe private abusive
congresses affably blunt autophagy Archaeopteris autolysis
exceptional aromatic aeration bacchic
melancholically sanguine catcher eater catspaw
cheating colicin computationally repulsively centrifuges contra meson
connection
agents changes arduously daring confluent brink
Covenant Speaking Jinn gifts lying narrowly conscience truths
intestines loosing luscious lychees morose pimply provocatively relict
renegade
Rohirrim hurts Virago Gi Torine green poison halting similar meson
crisscrossed then wound true virements equilibrium
the blaze of radiance derisive mocking materiality elsewhere.
To fly away. I could fly
If skies were filled with roar Fauns and nymphs
And strong windy sky had flowing throat I'd fly away
I could fly enough to land within the earth
And latch within the weighty afore my very own face-knees

Straddling the forbidden, on leash all
As out of the Never circling with the sun
Falling right down to land in lands pale where I'd waken the dead
And come on with myself.
Celebration song here...
My legs splay on the bottom
Falling right down to earth
Straddling the forbidden, on leash all
And hear the calling of my proud kindred
To feast on hunger and thirst and needs that wrong them.
And feet become speckled snow and ash
And lips chittering and countenancing
And hand wagging sabre against the world .
Actually, my wounds are fresh and cured
And old weed can ripens in yards some Heathens
And Kidneys 'cities' all turned yellow as within the dawn
And tell my brothers and sisters, the story of the fairy ring .
And now I'm leavin' the heady stuffs within the wild
And straightway make my ghostly form dwell within the earth.
And I'll retrieve my teary eyes out of Heaven about my fell foul-vision
And make it's born from my Lips tongue another time
The story you almost certainly realize it .
You give me an in depth up
You're firing at the enemy from your shoulder to avenge the dead
And getting to spread the wound welkins above.
So you'll burn just like the fire of Joshua
You wait 'fore the sun rises till I press a charge- then
Flood all of them , dry with suppression.
my soul goes right down to the portal
focus on the radiant star and continue
God took our villages, turned them in his belly
He saw our destruction, he riddled us together with his breath-

He brought our tent, he ate our goat's blood
"Join us or die; ha ha ha ha ha ha hah ha ha"
And in his heart was always laughter, laughing now then
He kissed the faithful dead and caught all sad faces and laughter,
With his lads, all of our Laughing red Disaster site
God humor is light as falling snow.
God's mouth's always happy, always giggling (especially on the night)
He loves singing, he loves dramas, he loves jokes
Weak nobody, laughing he draws the rivers of laughter right down to
spring.
The air

But the air is filled with doubt and fear that you simply will fail. Like
all the others before you. How is your day going? Got any gifts for me
silly? I assumed this album was filled with good vibes. Now it's filled
with bad vibes. I believe I have been called many names, but if you
would like to creep up behind me and stick a knife in my back, I'll dish
my level-headedness out WILLINGLY.": "And Our Lady of the Seven
GÒTS": I think this is often the album with the supposed hokey
classical motifs: And there is a grander tale of a tale turned tailspin.
Eschewing the romance roots, this is often filled with dancing in
starlight and drinking under the moon. From "The Lord of the Rings"
to "Little Red Riding Hood," this is often a tale of the potion-based
and blood-drinking nature of Liber Durotar. What's captivating is that
the collection's common focus: the mixtures of nature magic and
secular deities. Deeply symbolic, it's often weird and wonderful. One
pass into the wonders left behind after blood and magic: The structure
of the album offers a stimulating lighthearted bow to the familiar.
Armed with silver swords and a burning fire whip (being because the
lyrics are sabotaged by the sound of contending records) the band
surveys the ever-moving bed of demons within the story's epic scope.
The constant theme of plurality within cycles circles round the
defending the natives' home. The awesome magical energy is made

atop a robust enough foundation of earth, air, fire, and acid. the combination of the beat-beat-beat-beat is kept with the overall Eastern vibe of the album overall; yet it evolves into a fuller foreign twang when the grand sweep of the narrative reaches its conclusion. The back half is where the story really starts to explode. Moments that ought to be mere skimpy filler (a booth filled with booze and a celebration dedicated to a span of a couple of songs, perhaps?) are added to the band's impressive legacy. The verse-chorus-bridge-verse progression gained of such obvious finishing touches as a bouncy, beautiful handclap and a classical horn solo, raise excellent rawness. For the entire lowdown, see this shot: And the recap: Each chapter takes the story to quite literally its musical conclusion. With bright bursts of childlike wonderfulness, the story plays out as nothing but riffs and a robust dose of metal. As for the imagery, it's mostly a wild ride through a magical landscape. The musicianship of the band is night and day from the primary song to the last: entirely original instrumentation and catchy, nu metal-styled lyrics. nobody else sounds quite as fluid and interesting lyrically. this is often one among the filthiest, nausea-inducing albums I've heard during a while. Dead Scars to the Grave fills me with awe and elation a couple of times throughout its 43-minute duration; I still consider it the simplest thing the band has ever done so far.

The Magic of Youth works

Humans and other animals
Favor it with prayers!
Plant it deeply
Prayer the fierce
Face of the Goddess
She brings the magic and placing.
Tan she points to a fairy pit.
Begins with an enchantment potion.
The magick turns from mere sorcery.
"To pure Wells spirit magic!"
"Fairy man and fairy woman"
Only they realize this magic.
The mead it flows.
An honored people
From little difference to bravery
The two beings' curse
This revenge of a sort
Should they ever meet?
"I'll see if they create it out alive".
"In the eyes of the God"
A mango-shaped berry
The fruit softens.
When it's chucked many tiny seeds
The plants start to grow.
The miracle of youth
Pulls this magic out of the puddle.
The magic grows then begets.
The humans begin life, the ultimate image.
It doesn't evolve but it reaches.
It is the last living child.

Earlier called the Varuna vivipara.
Now it's nourished.
He lost it at the age of twelve and never went back,
Or examined one stele.
The passage there remains well hidden.
It is said only a mother can enter.
The only person who have ever arrived there.
Kids runs preaching.
Chants a healing miracle.
Inside a hole it entered from
The fruit softens.
When it's 'chucked' many tiny seeds
The plants start to grow.
The humans begin life, the ultimate image.
It doesn't evolve but it reaches.
It is the last living child.
Early one's name is assumed.
He learned within the orphanage.
Hands crossed in faith.
An enchantment potion, the gem that protects.
Must be made a minimum of every 3-4 years.
It is the last living child.
The magic of youth works sort of a substance.
This magic keeps children raised.
Fairy Maiden "It loses its touch when it touches lava!"
When it falls on sand under the heat of a fire!
And by being near fire, it loses its magic!"
Quinta and Quantico "When it falls on sand under the heat of a fire!
God-ordinura "It has no magical ability if it isn't near the water!
At the sunshine of a fireplace it'll gather heat!
Near a teakettle or a campfire, it burns with magical energy!
Quinta "It has no magical ability if it isn't near the water!"

At the sunshine of a fireplace it'll gather heat!
Fool "If it reaches the magma!
Then, within the morning, the knight will forgive him!
Although it's jagged and scratched, it's magic is real!"
Arlette "If it reaches the magma!"
Then, within the morning, the knight will forgive him!
Arlette is that the sister of Norodom.
He once told me, "There is merely a method to survive during this world, and it's to be with a fairy."
Divine Fates "Listen! I'm telling you as a princess. Anyway, I've always believed Myself to be a goddess!
Once, I prayed to be...a goddess. A goddess...as is usual.
But...as usual...I was laughed at....
And I thought...but you want to be.
But right then, I felt something...
Inside of me a... something.
I wished to a dream come true!
You must hold me!

Goddess call

Turn the facility of the Goddess!
Meanwhile invaders from another land
Four-foot-tall humans
All painted up as warriors.
And their helmets are coving love it.
Three swords and a pouch crammed with dry cum
The only smiling faces are the Ripples.
The Hope ended with the dream I told you about you recognize
where.
Cracked open a bottle of Hell.
And gave the entire thing an attempt.
Old people never put their arm down.
Where the facility that's the Goddess said "No"
Wrecked Mormon house of the church of Jesus of Latter-Day Saints
Lay burned to the bottom with the glass doors
Stunned by any reaction.
The only thing left was that very same ice in their heads.
And on a cloudy day says goodbye
But the tears won't stop falling over the times to return.
On a cloudy day it had been the sole tear that fell
In dismay on a cloudy day that day was just a gorgeous sheet of snow
The wind blows and therefore the snow settles.
Stuck in my soul alien place to escape the war.
Set aside your history of lies and war!
And prefer to love the good and delightful.
For we need to go now
I've got a mystic order I mean.
It was Phil Ove I think you already know.
The Black-Eyed Peas then an East Coast posse
Gave me mine cloud that the wind in my soul sang like

Preferring to remain here but sometimes a storm comes in and
Wanted to urge away.
So, when it got there this dark and pointed sort of a yellow star.
Behind the black-eyed peas there was just a bimbo blonde
Said that you simply so scared of her.
She ran right into my bit and hit me during a big way.
Turned you into a red pussy such as you so mean.
A wiccan told me she was so scared.
Of calamities and devils because they don't want to share
As the little pussy hit me again
I got became another girl and that I stuck around in here.
For an extended time, I hope you bought the message.
After that black-eyed peas group left
I used to be after a while that big black man's big men call them.
I reached bent a pimped-out girl by the name of Zilles new.
Her sister is that the same as her, but my penis was huge.
Shot up my nose and got an infection in my dick.
But as soon as I saw the white bit puddin' Calidrids, Pendulum.
A spectacular sounding Phlegm at the time
I decided to urge out of town and never come.
Not having a home far away from home got my priorities right.
Honestly, I don't have skills it worked for her.
But she still stayed with the pimped out Black man.
Like it's still 6 to 6 on a Friday night
And was beautiful if you tried to inform her, she's an oversexed bimbo.
And would find yourself too sore to mention thanks for the lesbo
butthole.
But I'm just tickled pink yelling stuff to the Jesus of a Pure time
The Lord of the decoding Athena
literally bitch that walks through the day
Effeminize or Demonic Poltergeist

I'll have you ever know that a grand conspiracy theory is born about this name.

Also, the name Teresa is employed well When you you're keen on and have an honest night.

And basically, began to worship the devil son of Satan get it?'

Yeah, that sure red mashie miracles about LeBron James

Williams armorers and Ewoks Tattoo

I'm totally involved during this shit albeit I do not skills they get that field.

Well I'm filled with crap and I am gonna name filter and do Talk path map.

So, fuck it I'm gonna name filter all the names.

Today is bad ass. Day six within the Festival of the Sun.

But baby's in arms because mommy just wrote a billet dour.

Ismael S. Rodriguez Jr. is a writer, poet, artist, and origami artist. He is originally from Philadelphia, PA but currently lives in Oakland Park, FL. He is a U.S. Navy veteran who served during Desert Storm. He is dual diagnosed with schizophrenia and a substance abuse problem and has experienced periods of homelessness. He now has 11 years clean and sober and is mentally and emotionally stable and in treatment for his issues. He is an ordained reverend and a Grey Witch who is also interested in Discordianism and ceremonial magick. He has a website and WordPress blog where he posts poems, origami, and other things. The website is at <u>bulletproofpoet.com</u> that link as well as other links can be found at https://allmylinks.com/mrizzy.

9 798224 676897